WINSLOW HOMER

WINSLOW HOMER

by Lloyd Goodrich

A&W Visual Library

Acknowledgements

THIS BOOK is published on the occasion of the Winslow Homer Retrospective Exhibition organized by the Whitney Museum of American Art in 1973, shown subsequently in the Los Angeles County Museum of Art and the Art Institute of Chicago. The exhibition was assisted by a public service grant from Champion International and its Champion Papers division, with additional assistance from the National Endowment for the Arts. The Whitney Museum wishes to record its gratitude to the two institutions for their support, which made the exhibition possible.

The Whitney Museum wishes to thank museums and collectors for their kind permission to reproduce works from their collections.

The Museum and the author express their gratitude to Mr. George Braziller for his permission to use portions of the text of *Winslow Homer* by the author, published by George Braziller. Inc., in 1959.

Contents

Winslow Homer

WINSLOW HOMER was a man of many works but few words. In his old age his future biographer William Howe Downes wrote him proposing a book, and received this characteristic reply: "I think that it would probably kill me to have such a thing appear, and as the most interesting part of my life is of no concern to the public I must decline to give you any particulars in regard to it." So whatever we know about Homer's life and mind must be found in contemporary accounts, not very numerous, and in his letters—but above all in his work, in which he left the fullest record of himself.

He was a New Englander by birth and long ancestry: the Homers had come from England to Massachusetts almost two centuries before he was born on February 24, 1836, in Boston. His family was middle-class. Brought up in nearby Cambridge, still not much more than a village, he had an active outdoor boyhood that left a lifelong preference for the country. He grew up to be an independent, strong-willed young man, hardworking and ambitious, reserved and taciturn but forthright in what he did say, and with a dry Yankee sense of humor.

Without any art instruction as far as we know, he was apprenticed at about nineteen to a leading Boston lithographic shop, John H. Bufford's, where he was marked by his skill in drawing. But he hated the drudgery of the job, and when he reached twenty-one he launched himself as a free-lance illustrator. *Harper's Weekly,* the best American illustrated magazine of the time, accepted his drawings from the first, and in 1859 he moved to New York, and was soon one of the *Weekly's* most popular artists. With the outbreak of the Civil War the magazine sent him several times to the Virginia front, where he drew innumerable sketches from which, back in New York, he composed his illustrations. Mostly of everyday life in camp rather than battles, their honest realism and strong draftsmanship made them the most authentic pictorial records (together with Mathew Brady's photographs) of how the average Civil War soldier really looked and acted.

But illustrating did not satisfy Homer. While still at Bufford's he had said to a fellow apprentice when they were in an art gallery, "I am going to paint"; asked what kind of work, he pointed to a picture by the French genre painter Edouard Frère and said, "Something like that, only a damned sight better." After moving to New York he attended "a drawing-school in Brooklyn" (name unknown) and at about twenty-five entered a night class of the National Academy of Design. American art schools of the time were meager: the Academy offered drawing from antique casts, and after months, possible admission to a life class where only drawing was taught, not painting. Not a scrap of Homer's student work has been found, and in all his known pictures there is only one nude study, made much later.

Homer's first chronicler, the critic George William Sheldon, wrote in 1878: "In 1861 he determined to paint. For a month...he took lessons in painting of Rondel, an artist from Boston, who once a week, on Saturdays, taught him how to handle his brush, set his palette, etc. The next summer he bought a tin box containing brushes, colors, oils, and various equipments and started out into the country to paint from Nature." (This Frédéric Rondel was a genre and landscape painter whose pictures, though old-fashioned, had enough quality to cause at least one of them in recent years, with a forged Homer signature, to be passed off as a Homer.)

Thus the extent of Homer's known art education was some drawing from casts and possibly from life, and four or five lessons by a minor artist in the elementary mechanics of painting. Everything else he learned for himself. Certainly if any artist can be called self-taught, he was. Obviously he was a natural draftsman; and his most valuable training was his experience as an illustrator. But this experience was in black and white, not in color.

He was twenty-six before he began to paint seriously—an unusually late start. But his first paintings, which were like his illustrations in their war subjects and their realism, revealed a technical ability remarkable in a man just beginning to use oils. In 1866 his *Prisoners from the Front,* now in the Metropolitan Museum, made his reputation as a painter; and thereafter, while often subject to adverse criticism and low finances, he was never neglected.

HOMER'S BOYHOOD LOVE of the outdoor world continued into adult life, growing and deepening with the years. After the Civil War, it furnished the main content of his art for the rest of his life. Though New York was his winter home for over twenty years, he never painted it and seldom illustrated it. (In this he was not alone; the ugly, chaotic American cities were not to become accepted subjects for artists until the turn of the century.) From late spring into the fall he worked in the country, in various places, mostly in New England but also in eastern New York state and New Jersey. It was these summer months that supplied material for almost all his early paintings and illustrations.

We usually think of Winslow Homer as the solitary of his later years in Maine. But the young Homer was different. Good-looking though not conventionally handsome, he was short

LEFT: *Cavalry Soldier.* 1863. Black chalk. 14¼ x 7-15/16.
Cooper-Hewitt Museum of Decorative Arts and Design.

RIGHT: *Zouave.* 1864. Black and white chalk. 16⅞ x 7½.
Cooper-Hewitt Museum of Decorative Arts and Design.

and lean, with dark hair, a strong aquiline nose, handlebar moustaches, and a poker face; and always neatly, even nattily dressed. Though far from hail-fellow-well-met he had many friends among his fellow artists. "He was a quiet little fellow, but he liked to be in the thick of things," said one friend; and another: "He had the usual number of love affairs when he was a young man."

That he admired feminine beauty and had an eye for fashion is demonstrated by his illustrations and paintings of the world of summer resorts at the seashore or in the mountains, with young women in the leading roles. In this age of increasing physical freedom they were no longer languishing Victorian females but outdoor girls, riding, picnicking, playing croquet—all in the voluminous crinolines, bustles, flounces, puffed sleeves, flying ribbons and other charming absurdities of that unstreamlined day. Always they were young and comely, with an air of mingled independence and innocence. He tended to make them types rather than individuals—the Homer Girl, like the Gibson Girl of the 1890s—but he did not idealize them into the ethereal creatures favored by his contemporaries. On the other hand, they were viewed with a certain aloofness, as attractive decorative figures rather than intimately seen human beings. Nevertheless he was

A Bivouac Fire on the Potomac. Wood-engraving. 13¾ x 20⅛. *Harper's Weekly,* December 21, 1861.

one of the first and most appreciative portrayers of contemporary American women, and his pictures of them are a delightful record of leisured outdoor life in the 1860s and 1870s.

The reverse side of rural life, the deep country and its natives, had as large a part in his work. The old-fashioned American farm had long been a favorite subject of genre painters, who usually depicted it with nostalgic idealization. Homer's attitude was more realistic; his farmers and country women with their homely figures and clothes, their bare wooden houses and barns, rail fences and tumbledown stone walls were portrayed with fidelity to their character. But beneath this realism was a deep attachment to the country and its people, to this life spent in intimate contact with the earth and the changing seasons. His rural pictures, with all their objectivity, revealed a warmth and depth of feeling not always present in his scenes of the leisured world. The character and flavor of American farm life had never been captured with more authenticity and love.

Children were the center of many of these scenes, helping with chores or more often busy with their own concerns. They were pictured with complete sympathy and understanding, but with no trace of the mawkish sentimentality common in genre of the period. Homer had preserved not only boyhood's enjoyment of the outdoors but boyhood's realism; his art is the world as a boy sees and feels it, realized with a man's grasp of actualities. These childhood scenes have an early-morning freshness, a sense of freedom in nature, of delights to be explored, such as we remember from our own young days in the country.

This self-identification with childhood was appearing also in American literature of these years. Our writers were attracted to the remembered golden age of youth more than to the Gilded Age of contemporary America. The 1860s and 1870s were producing such books as *Tom Sawyer* and *Little Women,* which often read like Homer's pictures put into words. But there was no element of nostalgia in his art; it was too actual for that—nearer the realism of Mark Twain than the sentiment of Longfellow.

Underlying Homer's naturalism was a vein of idyllic poetry, expressing itself not in subjective terms but in the exactness of his images of the things he loved. This combination of utter authenticity and reserved idyllicism gave his early work a unique flavor. It had the candor of youth, which was to disappear with the years and to be replaced by other qualities. His paintings and illustrations of the 1860s and 1870s, so different from his later works, form one of the most refreshing chapters in the history of American art.

HOMER'S work of these two decades was a continuation of the native genre tradition initiated in the 1830s by Mount and still being carried on by popular painters such as Wood, Guy and J. G. Brown with their sentimental or humorous storytelling pictures. But Homer's content marked a departure from the old school. Though his first paintings like his illustrations had a storytelling element, as time passed it was subordinated; he was no longer telling stories but

Winslow Homer, about 1880. Photograph by Sarony, New York.

presenting aspects of contemporary life in America. These works were not anecdotal; they did not depend on funny or touching situations. Even when young women and men were featured together, there was no sentimental confrontation: in *A Gloucester Farm* the girl is simply giving the boy a drink of water. Men and women and children were shown in their relation to nature, at work or play, with an emotional involvement that gave his art a depth and reality lacking in popular genre. Like his younger contemporary Thomas Eakins, Homer was bringing new dimensions to the old genre tradition.

His paintings of these years included few pure landscapes, and they were not his most interesting works. Mankind occupied the center of his scenes. But nature played an almost equal part. American landscape painting was then in its most grandiose phase, with the huge panoramic canvases of Church, Bierstadt and Moran representing the natural marvels of the continent. Homer's attitude was completely opposite: not Grand Canyons or volcanic eruptions, but the inhabited and cultivated countryside, intimately related to man. He did not even emphasize the changing aspects of this familiar world: stormy days, or sunsets, night or moonlight; almost always he pictured the light of ordinary day. The focus was on the facts of nature, not her moods.

From the beginning he worked a great deal outdoors. His paintings were obviously based on first-hand observation of visual reality. The very first ones were pure naturalism: photographic vision, uncompromising clarity, emphasis on local colors, insistent details, tight handling—a hard-boiled style. Within a year or so, however, his technique became broader, local colors were modified by light, and he learned to simplify. His style, with its freshness and directness, was that of a man who had looked at nature more than at other art. It had a quality as attractive as it was rare—an innocent eye. He was painting by eye, not by tradition; painting what he saw, not what he had been taught to see.

The exact effects of sunlight and outdoor color were carefully observed and accurately rendered. Lighted and shadowed areas were drawn with draftsmanlike precision. Most of his paintings represented full sunlight, with the sun high in the sky. Often the sun was somewhat in front of the viewer, so that the upper edges of figures were sunlit but their near sides in shadow— a device that made for an effective play of lights and darks. Yet with all this preoccupation with light, his general tonality in these early years was comparatively dark, and his color was on the warm side. But his tonal relations were true and the light in his pictures was well balanced.

Almost from the first Homer's style went beyond the bounds of literal naturalism. Whether consciously or unconsciously, for him colors and shapes were not only means of representation but had a sensuous life in themselves. He was alive to the purely physical properties of pigment and color, of line and form, and the patterns they created. A sense of pattern had appeared in some of his black and white illustrations; it was oddly suggestive of Japanese prints, with which he may have become acquainted through his friend John La Farge, who was collecting them in the early 1860s. This feeling for what might be called decorative values was clear in such

Homeward-bound. Wood-engraving. 13½ x 20½. *Harper's Weekly,* December 21, 1867.

a painting as *Croquet Scene* of 1866 with its flat areas of strong local colors, blue and scarlet and white, against the dark green of the grass and trees. It was a quality that distinguished his style from the literalism of the older American school.

Homer had a natural color sense, that gift that must be inborn and cannot be taught. Even though he did not use color until he was twenty-six, his command of chromatic relations and harmony was unexpectedly sophisticated. While relatively dark, his color had body, a sober strength, depth without sweetness. Its fine grays were given added value by knowledgeable use of positive notes.

For him, decorative values were not inconsistent with naturalism. He saw nature as both solid forms and simplified areas of color and tone, which involved no distortion of visual reality. As Henry James wrote in an otherwise negative review in 1875: "He sees not in lines, but in masses, in gross, broad masses. Things come already modelled to his eye." But in some paintings his naturalism predominated over his artistry. This conflict was to continue through much of his life: a recurring division between the claims of naturalism and of art, now one dominant, now the other; until in his later works he effected a synthesis of these two forces.

But Homer's gift was not merely for flat decorative values. His paintings were conceived in three dimensions; they created pictorial space occupied by round forms. In *The Morning Bell,* for example, the diagonals of the bridge and the dark woods converge toward the static mass of the mill in a finely balanced design. Out of familiar actualities he has created a satisfying design in depth. Not all his early compositions are as well constructed; some which are successful in other respects reveal inadequacies in design. It seems probable that he himself at this time was not fully aware of such matters. In this his pictures contrast with Thomas Eakins' similar genre paintings of the time, which were based on thorough scientific study of natural forms and of perspective. Homer's forms do not have the great substance of Eakins', and his three-dimensional space was not as completely comprehended. His gifts were wider, if not as deep.

WE KNOW VERY LITTLE about Homer's ideas on art. Few statements about art by him were recorded, and they were mostly about his subjects or purely representational problems. Many of his letters have been preserved, but aside from personal affairs they contain mostly business-like references to pictures under way.

The Beach at Long Branch. Wood-engraving. 12⅞ x 19½.
Appleton's Journal of Literature, Science and Art, August 21, 1869.

On the Bluff at Long Branch, at the Bathing Hour.
Wood-engraving. 8⅞ x 13¾.
Harper's Weekly, August 6, 1870.

"Winter"—A Skating Scene.
Wood-engraving. 9 x 13¾.
Harper's Weekly, January 25, 1868.

During his apprenticeship at Bufford's he had said to a fellow apprentice, "If a man wants to be an artist, he should never look at pictures." This can be put down to youthful bumptiousness, but it did represent something of his expressed attitude all his life. The dealer J. Eastman Chase, who knew him well from 1880 on, wrote: "Homer was less influenced by others and by what others had done than any artist—any man, I may as well say—I have ever known. He was a rare visitor to public galleries and exhibitions....Names meant little or nothing to him. He looked at any picture for precisely what it might have to say to him." And Homer's friend the critic Augustus Stonehouse wrote in 1887: "The difficulty he has shown in taking impressions of foreign art is almost ludicrous when comparisons are drawn between him and other workers."

With few artists is the favorite game of art scholars—detecting influences—less rewarding. We simply do not have enough firsthand evidence about his artistic contacts and tastes. As to his work, numerous ingenious surmises have been made by present-day writers, but many of them seem farfetched, based on tenuous evidence or on little more than similarity in subjects.

Yet the art of others, no matter how little he may have seen or thought of it, must have had some influence on him, since any artist's vision of reality and his manner of picturing it are conditioned to some degree by how others have pictured it, and by the general viewpoint of his time. To what degree, varies with the individual. In Homer's case, the testimony of all who knew him indicates that his degree of impressionability was minimal.

His early paintings, while related to the native genre school, were free from the outdated conventional style of most popular genre. Of all the school they were nearest to his older contemporaries Eastman Johnson and J. G. Brown, who were his fellow tenants in the Tenth Street Studios in New York. There are interesting parallels between Homer's style and that of Johnson in his informal pictures, and of Brown in his early ones. (The latter so much resemble Homer's work that recently an early Brown with a forged Homer signature was accepted as a Homer.) But the older painters, though sometimes displaying a visual freshness akin to Homer's, were basically traditional in style and technique.

Homer had a number of artist friends in the 1860s and 1870s, two of the closest being John La Farge and Homer Martin. These two became leaders in the anti-academic rebellion of the late 1870s called the New Movement, and were among the founders of the liberal Society of American Artists in 1877. But Homer took no part in the movement, never joined the Society, and did not exhibit with it until 1897. While he must have shared to some extent his friends' liberal viewpoint, they had no discernible influence on his style.

The chief foreign non-academic influence in America in the 1860s was that of the Barbizon school. La Farge later recalled that in those years he and Homer were interested in the Barbizon painters through their prints, then more available here than their paintings. Homer would doubtless have been in sympathy with their dedication to country life and nature's intimate aspects, and with their more or less naturalistic styles. But with the romantic and classic elements

Lumbering in Winter. Wood-engraving. 11¾ x 8¾.
Every Saturday, January 28, 1871.

in their work, Millet's religious and peasant moralism and Corot's classical side, he would have been less sympathetic. It was to the more naturalistic members of the school, Daubigny, Théodore Rousseau and Troyon, and to Corot in his phases of simple naturalism, that Homer's viewpoint was closest—closer than to the American academic establishment. His tonal and color range was much like theirs, and his visual directness was like Corot's. These relations were in general viewpoint rather than in specific style; there was nothing as explicit as the impress of Millet on Hunt or of Delacroix on La Farge—unmistakable influences, confirmed by the Americans themselves.

As much as with the Barbizon school Homer showed parallels with the young French impressionists: devotion to the contemporary scene, freedom from moral or literary content, concentration on outdoor light and color. But there were differences: Homer's rusticity, closer to Millet than to Monet, his identification with childhood, his lack of overt sexual content, and his avoidance of the urban scene that formed so essential an element in the French painters' world. Yet stylistically there are curious resemblances between certain of his early paintings and those of the impressionists, especially Monet. Homer's *Croquet Scene* of 1866 presents intriguing parallels with Monet's *Women in the Garden* of the same year, even to the extent of similar stylisms such as the simplified massing of lights and shadows, without modelling by halftones. But these parallels could not have resulted from influence, for Homer's picture was painted before he had been abroad and long before the French movement reached America. And the same characteristics had appeared in even earlier paintings by him. It is evident that he was a native precursor of impressionism, like Giovanni Fattori and the other Macchiaioli in Italy.

IT WAS NOT UNTIL the fall of 1866, when he was thirty, that Homer went abroad, spending ten months in France. He did not study in any art school, as far as we know, but painted on his own, mostly in the country; of his eighteen known French paintings, only a third were of Paris. (Where he spent at least part of his time in Paris is indicated by two *Harper's* illustrations of dance halls, subjects that Toulouse-Lautrec was to picture twenty years later.) Of what art he saw, he left no record. He did visit the Louvre, for a *Harper's* drawing shows the Long Gallery with student copyists (in the foreground, two Homer Girls). "He seems to have dealt little with the French artists," La Farge recalled, "...nor have I ever heard what he thought or said of the great masters' work. He might have been as silent upon that subject as on most." And Stonehouse wrote: "That obtuseness so unlike the alarming precocity of some American youths showed itself once more. He looked, he saw, doubtless he understood. But the character native to the man was too much for him....It is just this slowness to take suggestions that has made Mr. Homer, with all his limitations, the refreshing, the original artist he is."

The great Exposition Universelle opened in 1867. He had two paintings in the art section; and that he visited the fair is proved by his portrait of a woman perfume seller there. The

A Winter-morning—Shovelling Out.
Wood-engraving. 8¾ x 11¾.
Every Saturday, January 14, 1871.

Deer-stalking in the Adirondacks in Winter.
Wood-engraving. 8¾ x 11¾.
Every Saturday, January 21, 1871.

On the Beach—Two are Company, Three are None.
Wood-engraving. 9⅛ x 13¾.
Harper's Weekly, August 17, 1872.

Sea-side Sketches—A Clam-bake.
Wood-engraving. 9¼ x 14.
Harper's Weekly, August 28, 1873.

Raid on a Sand-swallow Colony—"How Many Eggs?". Wood-engraving.
13½ x 9⅛. *Harper's Weekly,* June 13, 1874.

Japanese had a pavilion, but it did not include an art exhibition; and in any case he could have seen Japanese prints back in America. Outside the Exposition grounds Courbet and Manet were holding large independent shows. He may have seen them, but there is no record that he did. His naturalism was in certain ways closer to Courbet's than to that of the Barbizon school, although the French realist's robust sensuality and the romantic survivals in his style were foreign to the American's temperament. (Homer's later marines and winter landscapes were to show parallels with Courbet's; but this was not until the 1890s.) Manet had not yet begun to paint outdoors, as Homer had, and his palette was still in the old-masterish range of his pre-impressionist period. The other future impressionists, of whom all but Pissarro and Degas were three or four years younger than Homer, had so far exhibited only sporadically; their first group exhibition was seven years in the future, as was the name "impressionist". It is possible that Homer met them or saw their work, but this is pure surmise.

Homer's own French paintings had less resemblance to impressionism than certain of his American ones; they were closer to the Barbizon school in their generally rustic subjects and quiet tonality; but they were not noticeably different from his earlier pictures. It was the paintings he did in the three years after his return, including *The Bridle Path, Long Branch* and *High Tide,* that were the closest to impressionism of all his early works. *The Bridle Path* with its high-keyed blond palette was his most luminous painting so far; the whole scene is bathed in light—direct sunlight, and reflected light from the rocks. In *Long Branch* the clear pale hues of the sea, cliffs and bathhouses show acute observation of the effect of midday sunlight on local colors; while the painting of the women's figures is as direct recording of visual sensations as by Monet. But the work that reveals the most thorough and accurate study of outdoor light and color is *High Tide;* not only direct sunlight but warm reflected light from the beach and cool light from the sky. Modelled by the interplay of these several lights, the figures stand out in sculptural roundness. Everything is distinct and sharp-edged, even the distant shore. Compared to impressionism, the picture is hard and a bit awkward; but it is as true to the light and color of a clear sunny noon as the impressionists' overemphasis on atmosphere. A searching, explorative work, not without faults, it was a remarkable achievement for an artist obviously working out complex problems on his own.

This luminous phase may have been stimulated by Homer's seeing French painting, which even in the Salons was higher in key than his previous work; or by the rediscovery of the stronger light and clearer air of his native country; or by both. In any case, it was not a permanent change; after three years his palette reverted at least partially to its former key, although through the 1870s he showed a growing skill in handling light. If he did encounter French impressionism in Paris, it had no such radical effect on him as on the younger generation of Americans. It was to be twenty years before the full-fledged French movement reached America in the persons of Weir, Robinson, Twachtman and Hassam.

In certain fundamental ways Homer's art differed from impressionism. To the true impressionist, light and atmosphere were as important as nature's solid substance; Monet said that he was painting not objects but the color of the air between him and them. But Homer's chief interest remained the object, the thing-in-itself. The impressionists bathed their scenes in luminous atmosphere, but his vision was always clear and precise. He never gave color as dominant a role; the structure of his pictures was based as much on values, in a full range from white down to darks much darker than the impressionists'. This, a continuation of his beginnings as a black and white artist, remained true of his style from first to last. As he said: "I have never tried to do anything but get the proper relationship of values." His color in the 1860s and 1870s was darker and warmer than the impressionists'; the shadows were never as cool, the distance as blue, and his palette included no such violets, mauves and blue-greens. And he never used the impressionist technique of divided tones.

Compared to the French impressionists' style of the same years, Homer's seems more literal and restrained. They were bolder in their innovations, more brilliant in color, more painterly. They were more sophisticated artists, heirs to a long tradition even though rebels against it. Homer had no such artistic background, and in comparison his art of these years seems limited and homespun. But in relation to established American painting it was innovative; and in the long run it was to expand in directions quite different from impressionism.

Homer's preoccupation with outdoor light is shown in a second article on him in 1880 by Sheldon, one of the few writers who got him to talk. "Almost everything that he has shown to the public...has been drawn directly from Nature," wrote Sheldon, "...No painter in this country, probably, has a profounder respect for such out-door work, a more lively apprehension of its value, or a sincerer and more serious aversion to manufactured and conventional studio-pictures. He paints what he has seen; he tells what he has felt; he records what he knows. Now, a painter who begins and finishes in-doors a figure of a man, woman, or child, that is out-doors, misses a hundred little facts, ...a hundred little accidental effects of sunshine and shadow that can be reproduced only in the immediate presence of Nature....Of Bouguereau, for instance, Mr. Homer says: 'I wouldn't go across the street to see a Bouguereau. His pictures look false; ... his light is not out-door light; his works are waxy and artificial. They are extremely near being frauds.' ... 'I prefer every time,' he says, 'a picture composed and painted out-doors....This making studies and then taking them home to use them is only half right. You get composition, but you lose freshness; you miss the subtle and, to the artist, the finer characteristics of the scene itself.... Out-doors you have the sky overhead giving one light; then the reflected light from whatever reflects; then the direct light of the sun; so that, in the blending and suffusing of these several luminations, there is no such thing as a line to be seen anywhere."

This, Homer's longest recorded statement on art, expressed a purely naturalistic philosophy. Yet Sheldon also wrote: "He believes, however, that the most complete pictures are not founded upon out-door studies. 'The great compositions of the old masters,' he says, 'were almost all interiors. You can't control the thing out-doors.' " Evidently at this time there was an unresolved conflict in Homer's mind between the claims of naturalistic truth and of what he called "composition".

UNTIL HE WAS almost forty Homer led a double life, as painter and illustrator. Almost all his illustrations were reproduced by wood-engraving. In this process the artist drew his picture on a fine-grained boxwood block, polished and coated with white. The block was then turned over to an engraver, who cut away the bare white areas, leaving the drawn lines in relief. The drawing itself had of course been destroyed in the process. The functions of artist and engraver were separate; as far as we know, Homer did not engrave his blocks.

Wood-engraving was essentially the same as printing from type; the relief surfaces printed and the impression was in flat black. Tones were translated by the engraver into minute parallel lines. The flatness of the medium offered decorative possibilities to artists who understood its physical nature. Homer was such an artist. While he used tone, his illustrations were built on

The Wreck of the Atlantic—Cast up by the Sea. Wood-engraving.
9⅛ x 13¾. *Harper's Weekly,* April 26, 1873.

a strong linear foundation; outlines were decided, and lights and darks were precisely defined. His wood-engravings often achieved handsome patterning; sometimes, as we have seen, suggesting Japanese prints, to which they were related in technique. On the other hand, the translation of his drawings into the engraver's lines inevitably resulted in some deadening of graphic quality, and one can speculate how much livelier his illustrations might have been if he had engraved them himself.

With the years they ceased to be illustrations in the usual sense; no longer reportorial or related to a written text, they became independent works of art. Often they were based on works already executed in other mediums, oils, watercolors and drawings, and frequently they combined elements from several such works to produce compositions more complete than the sources. Homer was a prolific artist, but also an economical one, and usable material was not wasted by him. His finest illustrations, such as the series in *Every Saturday* in 1870 and 1871 and in *Harper's Weekly* in 1873 and 1874, were among the best designed of all his works.

At the height of his popularity as an illustrator, in 1875, he stopped. His reasons, like so much in his personal life, are unknown. The most probable is that he had taken up a new

Gathering Berries. Wood-engraving. 9 x 13½. *Harper's Weekly,* July 11, 1874.

medium, watercolor, and was having some success in it. It is a curious fact that he was thirty-seven before he began working in this medium, of which he was to become one of the nineteenth-century masters. A collection of English watercolors shown at the National Academy in 1873 may have stimulated his interest. He devoted that summer, in Gloucester, Massachusetts, to a whole series of watercolors of children playing in the harbor and on the waterfront. Among all his works these first watercolors have a special quality. They have the freshness of life's morning; they are his purest expression of childhood's pleasure in summer and sunlight and the sea.

Watercolor suited Homer perfectly from the first. In it he could work from nature and produce a finished picture in one sitting. In watercolor he was to make the discoveries—of places and subjects, light and color—that he later embodied in oil. The translucency of the medium, with the white paper a basis for the washes, made an immediate difference in his color, which attained a new clarity and luminosity. The freshness and freedom of his watercolors anticipated later developments in his paintings.

Once started on watercolor he made it a medium as important as oil. Often he would devote to it most of his time in any one place, producing a series of similar subjects. One series painted in the summer of 1878 in Mountainville, New York, concentrated on half-grown girls and boys tending sheep or resting under the shade of trees. Sometimes the girls, instead of their everyday aprons and sunbonnets, were oddly arrayed in eighteenth-century costumes. Perhaps this was the effect on even Winslow Homer of the Centennial Exhibition of 1876, which revived interest in everything Colonial. But his adolescents wore their finery with a touch of native gawkiness, showing that he had not lost his sharp-eyed truthfulness. The result was an engaging blend of awkwardness and grace, of realism and rococo.

DURING THE 1870s Homer's art gained steadily in strength and skill. The experimental, tentative quality of some of his early work gave way to increasing sureness. The remaining traces of artistic naiveté disappeared. There was a growing command of light and its relation to form and space. His compositions took in more elements, and were more consciously and successfully designed.

His earlier themes continued, but with changes in viewpoint and emphasis. His works of the 1870s, as in former years, were much preoccupied with women. But his attitude was less remote. The athletic miss was less in evidence, and these young ladies were picking flowers, catching butterflies, reposing in hammocks, reading novels, embroidering, and engaged in other gentle female occupations, or simply sitting in revery. Often they were shown singly, as individuals instead of parts of a scene. The note of sentiment was clearer but still reserved, implicit rather than explicit: an appreciation of feminine grace but no emotional situations. Though more intimate, the artist's attitude was far from sensual. Sometimes these pictures bordered on sweetness, but their unmistakable reality kept them from going over the border. Still not idealized, his women were portrayed with a sensitivity to individual character that

Flamborough Head, England. 1882. Charcoal, pencil and Chinese white. 17½ x 24.
The Art Institute of Chicago, Mr. and Mrs. Martin A. Ryerson Collection.

might have made him an accomplished portraitist. His watercolors in particular were subtler and more refined than anything he had done before in the medium, with interesting parallels to Eakins' domestic watercolors of a few years later.

New kinds of subjects appeared in these years. One was Negro life. His interest in the black people dated back to the Civil War. In 1875 he revisited Petersburg, Virginia, and spent most of his time painting in the colored section. Most artists who had pictured the black man, with honorable exceptions such as Mount and Johnson, had made him a figure of fun. Homer took him seriously. In *The Cotton Pickers* he gave the women dignity and physical beauty. Humor was not absent, but a sympathetic humor, as in *The Carnival,* in which two women are sewing up a young buck in a brilliant pierrot costume. The contrast of dark skin and particolored clothes, seen under strong sunlight that picks out the bright notes, reveals a color sense rich in sophisticated juxapositions and harmonies.

At the same time that he was painting his feminine themes Homer was discovering a new world of masculine subjects. As early as 1870 he visited the Adirondacks, still largely wilderness; and in two versions of *An Adirondack Lake* he first embodied the love of wild nature that was to find full expression in later years. In the meantime, it produced some notable works. *The Two Guides* was one of his most fully realized paintings so far. The fine precision of details, from the keen characterization of the mountaineers down to the wild flowers in the foreground, does not detract from the breadth of conception and the sense of space and clear air and all-pervading light. In the handling of light playing on solid forms it was his most advanced work, almost photographically exact yet completely alive throughout. In these respects it challenges comparison with Degas' landscapes of this time. Here was fresh subject matter, a foretaste of Homer's work of fifteen years later. The contrast with his pictures of women reveals a growing

Figures on a Rock. c. 1882. Charcoal and white chalk.
21½ x 29¼. Collection of Huntington Hartford.

Two Fisherwomen. 1884. Charcoal and white chalk. 23 x 17⅜.
Collection of Mrs. James Lippincott Goodwin.

division in his aims: between the masculine and the feminine in subject, and between energy and refinement in style.

WHEN HE WAS FORTY-FIVE, in the spring of 1881, Homer made a second visit abroad that had a deeper effect than his stay in France fifteen years before. This time he went to England and spent two seasons near the fishing port of Tynemouth on the North Sea. Here he first began to paint the sea, and the men and women who wrested their living from it. Concentrating almost entirely on watercolor and drawing, he made scores of pictures of the fisherfolk, particularly the women. His fashionable young ladies were things of the past; these fishwives were sturdy women who did a man's work in unloading the boats and mending nets. This part of the East Coast was noted for its storms and shipwrecks, and his work showed a new awareness of the power and danger of the sea. His scenes were no longer sunlit, the sky no longer clear but a moving spectacle of clouds, the sea no longer the quiet water of Gloucester harbor but a threatening or raging element. There was a new sense of the drama of nature's shifting moods.

In England his style underwent a change—the greatest so far. He may have seen watercolors by English artists, a medium in which they had always excelled. (He himself exhibited a Tynemouth oil in the Royal Academy in 1882.) More indisputable influences were the English air, softening outlines and subduing colors, and the climate of the East Coast with its somber skies and gray northern light. Hard edges and flat passages gave way to rounder modelling; there was more envelopment by atmosphere; his color, while often dark, added a wide variety of grays, and a new depth and body; his technical skill increased; and his watercolors were filled with the movement of wind and wave and cloud. Most of them were evidently painted from life, outdoors; but a few large watercolors, in which his fisherwomen were given an heroic, statuesque character, were obviously done in his studio. These were his most consciously composed works so far, and impressive in a somewhat conventional style.

HOMER WAS SLOW to mature; he did not reach his full growth until long after most artists. Forty-five when he went to England, he was to be almost fifty when he found the path he was to follow, and fifty-four when his art began to reach its full stature. But in compensation he kept on growing to the end of his life; the works of his last fifteen years showed a steadily increasing power and artistry.

A year after his return from England, in 1883, he left New York for good and settled on the Maine coast at Prout's Neck, a lonely, rocky peninsula jutting out into the Atlantic, with cliffs against which the surf broke spectacularly in storms. Like all the coast of Maine it had the ruggedness of land that had fought the sea for thousands of years. In the 1880s only a few fishermen and farmers lived there, on the landward side. Homer built a studio on the high shore only a few hundred feet from the ocean; and this was to be his home for the rest of his

Foreground Study: Tree Roots, Prout's Neck.
Probably 1884.
Charcoal and white chalk. 15 ⅝ x 22 ⅞.
Cooper-Hewitt Museum of Decorative Arts and Design.

The Smuggler of Prout's Neck. 1884.
Charcoal and white chalk. 15 x 23.
Private Collection, courtesy of Vose Galleries.

Fishermen on Shore. 1884.
Charcoal and white chalk. 12¾ x 22¾.
The Montclair Art Museum.

Mackerel Fishing. 1884.
Charcoal and white chalk. 14½ x 23½.
Private Collection.

The Herring Net, or A Good Haul. Probably 1884. Black, brown and white chalk.
16⅝ x 20⅝. Cooper-Hewitt Museum of Decorative Arts and Design.

life. He lived alone, doing his own cooking and most of his housework. Winters he would occasionally visit Boston or New York, or some years go south. But often he spent the whole winter in Maine.

If he ever divulged what lay behind his withdrawal, there is no record of it. (Sometimes he said that he left New York to escape jury duty—a characteristic piece of leg-pulling.) There may have been personal factors that will never be known. After his death there was a family legend of a serious love affair, probably in his late thirties, which ended unhappily. This has since been denied by other members of his family. So the whole question of his personal relations with women, like so much in his life, remains unanswered.

But other factors, less questionable, lay in his character and his relation to society. He had never liked the city. He had loved nature as much as man. Now his center of interest had moved from inhabited to wild nature—to the sea, the forest and the mountains, and the men who were part of them. He had finally found the subjects that meant most to him, and the kind of life that would bring him closest to them.

There was no element of defeat or bitterness in this. His most intimate letters, to his elder brother Charles and the latter's wife, prove that his life in Maine was genuinely and deeply satisfying. "This is the only life in which I am permitted to mind my own business," he wrote. "I suppose I am today the only man in New England who can do it." And again: "The life that I have chosen gives me my full hours of enjoyment for the balance of my life. The Sun will not rise, or set, without my notice, and thanks."

From this time his art changed fundamentally. The idyllic worlds of leisure, the farm, and childhood disappeared. Women appeared less and less. He had turned his back on contemporary society. This might be called escape; but while others escaped into idealization or the past or subjective fantasy, Homer as usual continued to draw on actual life—but actual life on the simplest, most elemental level.

The first products of this change were a series of sea paintings dealing with men and the sea: *The Life Line, The Herring Net, The Fog Warning, Lost on the Grand Banks, Undertow* and *Eight Bells*. Their recurring theme was the peril of the sea and the drama of man's battle with it. In some of these pictures the storytelling element played a larger part than in any previous works. But they were not literary; they spoke in purely pictorial terms; and they had none of the sentimentality or triviality of most storytelling pictures of the time. Their content had elemental human meaning: man's strength and courage pitted against the forces of nature. Their dramatic force and realistic power soon won them a permanent place among pictorial epics of the sea. And they established Homer's reputation as one of the foremost American painters.

An equally far-reaching change took place in his style. The strain of feminine refinement in some earlier pictures was replaced by masculine power. The scale of his pictures grew larger. His technical skill increased phenomenally. His command of the human body, of the forms and movements of waves, of weather and light, showed a technical ability he had never attained before. On the other hand, this gain was not always matched by a gain in more purely artistic qualities. Certain of the new works were able pieces of naturalism but comparatively deficient in the freshness of vision and the sensuous appeal of color and handling that had marked the best of his earlier works. But this was to prove a temporary phase.

The few women who were to appear in Homer's paintings from this time on were robust outdoor types reminiscent of his Tynemouth fishwives, with hardly a trace of femininity. They were seen without either sentiment or sensuousness. One thinks of the sensual richness of Courbet and Renoir, the flesh-and-blood humanity of Eakins, and one sees that with Homer, sexual emotion, one of the motivating forces of art, had become sublimated, and all his great vitality was now channeled into the celebration of nature. To this comparative sexlessness, which also characterized much American art of the time, we can ascribe certain of his limitations as a plastic artist.

WHILE PAINTING his sea pieces Homer embarked on a new medium, etching. The eight plates he etched between 1884 and 1889 were all (except one) based on his sea paintings and his English watercolors. Doubtless he was motivated by the popularity of these works and a desire to reach a wider audience. But his etchings were not merely reproductions of his paintings; in every one he made changes that strengthened the composition: increasing the scale of the figures in relation to the whole, concentrating on the central elements, and eliminating non-essentials. In his largest plate, *Saved,* he so transformed the original composition of *The Life Line* as to make the etching a new creation, and one of his most effective designs.

Eight Bells. 1887. Etching. 19⅜ x 25. The Metropolitan Museum of Art.

40

His etchings were constructed primarily in pure line, including linear modelling, without relying on the complex methods of wiping and printing employed by the Whistler school. Compared to them his style was severe and hard. But no other American printmaker of the time had his structural strength, mastery of the human figure, and completeness of design. Indeed, his etchings had a sculptural quality beyond all but a few of his oils up to that time. They were among his most fully realized works in any medium. Homer himself thought so, for in a letter of 1902 he called his best new watercolors "as good work, with the exception of one or two etchings, as I ever did".

As the years passed at Prout's Neck, Homer's solitary life face-to-face with the Atlantic brought further changes in his art. Humanity appeared less frequently, and his theme became the sea itself. The drama of man's struggle with it was transformed into the drama of the ocean and its never-ending battle with the land.

It was the sea at its stormiest that he loved. Summer days of sunshine and blue water, favorite mood of the American impressionists, did not interest him; one such day he called the ocean "that duck pond down there". But when skies threatened and the wind rose and the great waves came swinging in to hurl themselves against the cliffs, he was in his element.

Most previous American marine painters had pictured the sea romantically, as a spectacle of conventionally curling waves. But Homer takes us right into the battlefront between sea and shore. He makes us feel the weight and power of the wave, the solidity of the rock, the impact of their collision. In other moods he gives us the mighty rhythmic flow of the tides, and the radiance of dawn and sunset over the moving waters. His marines are unique embodiments of the power, the danger and the beauty of the sea. Their closest counterparts in nineteenth-century painting are Courbet's sea pieces, which are romantic and traditional, whereas Homer's are realistic, conveying immediate physical sensations with maximum force. Their vitality and energy were new notes in American painting of the 1890s.

The loneliness and rigor of Prout's Neck in winter are suggested in laconic phrases in Homer's letters: "Night before last it was twelve below zero." "My nearest neighbor is half a mile away." "I am under a snow bank most of the time." These long Maine winters produced some of his most poignant works: snow-covered cliffs, rocks sheathed in ice, a leaden sea under a leaden sky. Most American landscape of the time was devoted to nature's smiling moods. Homer preferred her wild and lonely aspects. To him nature was a theater of contending forces. In all this he harked back to the Hudson River school, but with their romanticism replaced by vivid naturalism. In a day of prevailing feminine landscape painting, his was masculine and dynamic.

Among these winter scenes is his largest and one of his greatest paintings, *The Fox Hunt.* In the hard Maine winters a flock of starved crows would sometimes attack a fox. Here is no sign

Mending the Tears. 1888. Etching. 17⅜ x 23. The Metropolitan Museum of Art.

of man or his works; this primitive struggle is an unforgettable image of northern solitude. *The Fox Hunt* combines strong naturalism with a highly developed command of pattern, color harmony, and space relations. In this and other paintings of the 1890s he regained the artistry of many of his earlier works, but with greater structural strength and subtlety.

IN HIS SEASCAPES and landscapes Homer paid full attention to exact effects of weather, light and time of day. Of his *West Point, Prout's Neck* he wrote: "The picture is painted *fifteen minutes* after sunset—not one minute before—as up to that minute the clouds over the sun would have their edges lighted with a brilliant glow of color—but now (in this picture) the sun has got beyond their immediate range & *they are in shadow.* The light is from the sky in this picture. You can see that it took many days of careful observation to get this, (with a high sea & tide just right)."

Such meteorological accuracy again recalls impressionism. But he still differed from it in not subordinating nature's physical existence to her appearances, and in seeing her in terms of dynamic forces rather than as purely visual phenomena. In these respects his viewpoint was somewhere between Courbet and the impressionists: between the former's substance and the latters' concentration on nature's changing spectacle.

As we have seen, Homer's few recorded statements about art indicate that his expressed philosophy was wholly naturalistic: painting was primarily realistic representation. That this viewpoint did not change is revealed by his talks in 1903 with his friend John W. Beatty of the Carnegie Institute. Asked by Beatty if he ever "took the liberty" of modifying nature's colors, he replied: "Never! When I have selected the thing carefully, I paint it exactly as it appears." Of course he did not really do this, since it is impossible for the human hand to represent anything "exactly as it appears" without the human mind entering the picture, even if unconsciously.

Perils of the Sea. 1888. Etching. 16½ x 22. The Metropolitan Museum of Art.

43

Actually, Homer's work itself gives ample evidence of conscious artistic intent. In the first place, he was extremely selective. The revealing photographs taken by Philip C. Beam of the scenes of Homer's Prout's Neck paintings show how he simplified, eliminating non-essentials and concentrating on the large elements. This bigness of style had been instinctive from the first; as he matured it became deliberate. "Never put more than two waves in a picture; it's fussy," he once said. One has only to compare him with later academic marine specialists to see the difference between undiscriminating photography and highly selective art.

As we have seen, at various times and in some works the claims of naturalistic representation had been reconciled with those of design; in other works naturalism had predominated. As he matured, his artistry, his realization of the painting as not only representation but creation of design in sensuous terms, became increasingly conscious. In his finest mature paintings the balance of masses, the strong linear rhythms, the robust earthy color harmonies, were evidently the product of well-considered design. This was painting deeply rooted in the senses, as all vital art is, and also consciously controlled. In these mature works the two main strands of his artistic

Saved. 1889. Etching. 22⅞ x 32¾. The Metropolitan Museum of Art.
Photograph courtesy of Sotheby Parke Bernet, Inc.

character, naturalism and design, achieved a synthesis—the culmination of a long growth from instinctive to conscious artistry.

It is true that his gifts were more for two-dimensional and spatial design than for the deepest kind of plastic design. Consider for example his oils in which he undertook the ambitious subject of large-scale figures in action, outdoors. There is no question that the vitality of these works rank them among the strongest figure paintings in American art. But if we compare them with, for example, Géricault's *Raft of the Medusa,* we see that they do not reveal the quality that marks the greatest plastic creators: that passion for form which translates the forms of nature into pure art form. Homer cannot be numbered among the small company of these supreme formal composers, but rather in the larger but still high company of artists who combine strong naturalism with command of pattern and pictorial space. That he himself may have come to realize these gifts and limitations is suggested by the fact that in later years he did not often attempt complex figure compositions but concentrated on the kind of design of which he was a master.

HOMER'S PUREST artistic achievements, aside from his mature oils, were his later watercolors. Most of them were painted away from Prout's Neck. Almost every year he and his brother Charles, both experienced fishermen and hunters, made camping trips to the northern woods, at first the Adirondacks, later Quebec. Homer combined sport and art, painting scores of watercolors. For subjects he had all the forest and its life, animal and human. As in his earlier work, the central theme was nature and man; but now wild nature with its shy creatures, and men who seemed part of nature.

The wilderness had long been a favorite theme for American painters. The Hudson River school had painted it with a combination of spectacular romanticism and meticulous literalism. Homer's approach was radically different: that of a woodsman rather than a romantic poet. He expressed not subjective sentiments but physical sensations. By the immediacy of his art he conveyed the sensations of forest stillness, dark lake water broken by the splash of a leaping fish, the grace of deer, the exhilaration of the mountaintop, the somber coldness of northern skies, the wild beauty of all this unspoiled world. Never had his art been closer to its primal source, nature. In these works he captured the virgin freshness of the American wilderness as few artists had.

Most previous American watercolor had remained, essentially, colored drawing. Homer brought to the medium a basically new style: painterly handling, full-bodied color. He was painting as purely by eye as in earlier years, but with an eye and a hand far more experienced. He drew with the brush, freely yet with complete control. Mostly painted on the spot, directly from the motif, these watercolors were nevertheless composed with unerring rightness of design. Their linear beauty, their handsomeness of pattern, and their deep, resonant color harmonies place them among his major achievements.

From the late 1890s Homer spent part of most winters in the Bahamas, Florida or Bermuda. The Bahama Islands opened up to him a new world of light and color. In this outwardly dry, matter-of-fact Yankee appeared an unexpected strain of paganism, of delight in the beauty of the islands and their people. The free primitive life of the Bahamians was pictured in a series of superb watercolors: stalwart young black men diving for sponges, catching sea turtles, tending their white fishing sloops; and by contrast with these sunbaked idylls, a tropical hurricane and its aftermath, a boy's body cast up on the beach beside his smashed boat. With all their realism, these works have a pagan spirit akin to Greek art. It is noteworthy that Homer was in his middle sixties when he painted these watercolors, so young in their vitality and their simple physical power. (It was in these years that Gauguin was also discovering his earthly paradise in the South Seas, and experiencing a similar liberation in color; but even the most avid seeker for influences would find it hard to link these two.)

Homer's watercolors were always in advance of his oils in color and in freedom of handling. The oil medium offers richer technical possibilities in the way of underpainting and glazes, but like most of his generation, Homer's oil technique remained relatively direct: masterly and rich within its limits, but not realizing the full depth of which the medium is capable. In watercolor, however, he made full use of the translucency that is the special beauty of the medium. He knew all the tricks of the craft, but he never depended on technical display, as did Sargent: his water-colors have the same kind of solid substance as his oils.

His later watercolors, whether northern or southern, are the purest manifestation in all his work of the visual sensuousness that is one of the most vital elements in his art. They contain the essence of his genius: the direct impact of nature on the eye, recorded in its purity by the hand of a master. He himself was well aware of their quality, for he once said, "You will see, in the future I will live by my watercolors." His last dated watercolor, *Diamond Shoal* of 1905, shows his power undiminished.

His southern trips resulted in his most famous oil, *The Gulf Stream.* This painting of a Bahamian lying on the deck of his dismasted boat, waiting apathetically for inevitable death, is the last and most powerful version of his recurring theme, the peril of the sea—but this time with an added irony in the tropical sunlight and the deep blue southern sea. A group of school teachers once asked his dealer, Knoedler's, for an explanation of the subject, and Homer wrote: "You can tell these ladies that the unfortunate negro who now is so dazed & parboiled, will be rescued & returned to his friends and home, & ever after live happily."

HOMER ACHIEVED recognition early, although never the financial success of an international favorite like Sargent. All his important oils were sold during his lifetime. In his old age he was generally considered the foremost painter living in America, and he received many honors. None of this made any difference in his solitary way of living, or in the quantity or quality of his works. He died in his studio at Prout's Neck on September 29, 1910, aged seventy-four.

Two Men in a Canoe. 1895. Monochrome watercolor.
13-3/16 x 19⅜. Private Collection.

Three Men in a Canoe. 1895. Monochrome watercolor.
13¾ x 19¾. Collection of Mrs. Wellington Henderson.

In his long, active career Winslow Homer developed from a native genre painter into the greatest pictorial poet of outdoor life in America. Through the years his art evolved from naturalism to conscious artistry. In his energy, the pristine freshness of his vision, and his simple sensuous vitality, he expressed certain aspects of the American spirit as no preceding artist had. His evolution epitomizes the growth of American painting in the second half of the nineteenth century, from provincial limitations to the main stream of world art.

Oils and Watercolors

The Initials. 1864. Oil. 15½ x 11½.
Collection of Dr. and Mrs. Irving Levitt.

Home, Sweet Home. Probably 1863. Oil. 21⅝ x 16⅜.
Collection of Mr. and Mrs. Nathan Shaye.

51

The Bright Side. 1865. Oil. 13 x 17½. Private Collection.

Pitching Quoits. 1865. Oil. 26¾ x 53⅝. Fogg Art Museum.

The Morning Bell. c. 1866. Oil. 24 x 38. Yale University Art Gallery.

Croquet Scene. 1866. Oil. 16 x 26. The Art Institute of Chicago.

The Nurse. 1867. Oil on wood. 19 x 11.
Collection of Mrs. Norman B. Woolworth.

The Country School. 1871. Oil. 21⅜ x 38⅜. The St. Louis Art Museum.

The Bridle Path, White Mountains. 1868. Oil. 24⅛ x 38. Sterling and Francine Clark Art Institute.

Long Branch. 1869. Oil. 16 x 21½. Museum of Fine Arts, Boston.

OPPOSITE, ABOVE: *On the Beach.* c. 1870. Oil. 15 x 24½. Canajoharie Library and Art Gallery.
OPPOSITE, BELOW: *Beach Scene.* c. 1870. Oil. 11¼ x 10¼. Private Collection.

An Adirondack Lake. 1870. Oil. 24 x 38. Henry Gallery, University of Washington.

Crossing the Pasture. c. 1872. Oil. 26 x 38. Private Collection.

Snap the Whip. 1872. Oil. 22¼ x 36½. The Butler Institute of American Art.

Grace Hoops. 1872. Oil. 22½ x 15½. Collection of Thomas M. Evans.

Dad's Coming. 1873. Oil on wood. 9 x 13¾. Collection of Mr. and Mrs. Paul Mellon.

Three Boys on the Shore. 1873. Watercolor. 8¼ x 14. Collection of Mr. and Mrs. Maximilian Agassiz Tufts.

The Farm Yard Wall. c. 1873. Watercolor. 7⅝ x 13½. Collection of G. Frederick Stork.

A Basket of Clams. 1873. Watercolor. 11⅜ x 9⅞. Collection of Mr. and Mrs. Arthur G. Altschul.

Whittling Boy. 1873. Oil. 15 ½ x 22 ⅝. Malden Public Library.

The Dinner Horn. 1873. Oil. 11 ⅞ x 14 ¼. The Detroit Institute of Arts.

Enchanted. 1874. Oil. 12 x 20. Collection of Mrs. Harold F. Wendel.

OPPOSITE, ABOVE: *Children Sitting on a Fence.* 1874. Watercolor. 6¾ x 11½. Williams College Museum of Art.
OPPOSITE, BELOW: *The Busy Bee.* 1875. Watercolor. 9⅜ x 8⅞. Timken Art Gallery.

Weaning the Calf. 1875. Oil. 24 x 38. The North Carolina Museum of Art.

Milking Time. 1875. Oil. 24 x 38. Delaware Art Museum.

The Trysting Place. 1875. Watercolor.
13⅞ x 8⅛. Princeton University Library.

What Is It? 1875. Watercolor. 9½ x 13⅜.
Collection of Mrs. Harry Rubin.

Rustic Courtship, or In the Garden. 1874.
Watercolor. 8⅝ x 12¼.
Private Collection.

The Two Guides. 1876. Oil. 24¼ x 38¼. Sterling and Francine Clark Art Institute.

Breezing Up, or A Fair Wind. 1876. Oil. 24⅛ x 38⅛. National Gallery of Art.

The Watermelon Boys. 1876. Oil. 24⅛ x 38¼. Cooper-Hewitt Museum of Decorative Arts and Design.

The Carnival. 1877. Oil. 20 x 30. The Metropolitan Museum of Art.

In the Mountains. 1877. Oil. 24 x 38. The Brooklyn Museum.

OPPOSITE: *Autumn.* 1877. Oil. 38¼ x 24¼. Collection of Mr. and Mrs. Paul Mellon.

Butterflies. 1878. Oil. 38 x 24.
The New Britain Museum of American Art.

Gathering Autumn Leaves. c. 1877.
Oil. 38¼ x 24¼.
Cooper-Hewitt Museum of Decorative Arts and Design.

Spring. 1878. Watercolor. 11⅛ x 8⅝. The Rita and Daniel Fraad Collection.

Fresh Air. 1878. Watercolor. 20¼ x 13¾. The Brooklyn Museum.

Looking Over the Cliff. 1882. Watercolor. 20½ x 13½. Plainfield Public Library.

OPPOSITE, ABOVE: *Woman with a Flower.* 1880. Watercolor. 8¾ x 11¼. Collection of Mr. and Mrs. Arthur G. Altschul.
OPPOSITE, BELOW: *Harrowing.* 1879. Watercolor. 12 x 19. Collection of Mr. and Mrs. James W. Titelman.

The Wreck of the Iron Crown. 1881. Watercolor. 20¼ x 29⅜. Collection of Carleton Mitchell.

Fishwives. 1883. Watercolor. 18¼ x 29½. The Currier Gallery of Art.

A Voice from the Cliffs. 1883. Watercolor. 20¾ x 29¾. Collection of Mrs. Charlotte M. Ford.

A Swell of the Ocean. 1883.
Watercolor. 14 x 20⅜. Private Collection.

The Wreck, or Girl with Red Stockings. 1882.
Watercolor. 13¼ x 19-3/16.
Museum of Fine Arts, Boston.

The Herring Net. 1885. Oil. 30¼ x 48½. *The Art Institute of Chicago.*

Lost on the Grand Banks. 1885-86. Oil. 28¼ x 48¼. Collection of Mr. and Mrs. John S. Broome.

Undertow. 1886. Oil. 29-13/16 x 47⅝. Sterling and Francine Clark Art Institute.

Shark Fishing—Nassau Bar. Probably 1885.
Watercolor. 13⅞ x 20.
Collection of Mr. and Mrs. Laurance S. Rockefeller.

Conch Divers. 1885.
Watercolor. 14 x 20.
The Minneapolis Institute of Arts.

A "Norther", Key West. Probably 1886.
Watercolor. 14 x 20. Private Collection.

Cabins, Nassau. 1885. Watercolor.
13½ x 19½. Collection of George deF. Lord.

Florida Palms. 1886. Watercolor. 16 x 13. Collection of Barbara B. Lassiter.

Boy Fishing. 1892. Watercolor. 14⅝ x 21.
Collection of Anthony T. Ladd, M.D.

Leaping Trout. Probably 1889.
Watercolor. 14 x 20. Museum of Fine Arts, Boston.

Huntsman and Dogs. 1891. Oil. 28¼ x 48. Commissioners of Fairmount Park, William L. Elkins Collection, Courtesy of the Philadelphia Museum of Art.

Deer Drinking. 1892. Watercolor. 13½ x 19½. Private Collection.

After the Hunt. 1892. Watercolor. 13¾ x 19¾. Los Angeles County Museum of Art, Paul Rodman Mabury Collection.

A Good Shot. 1892. Watercolor. 14½ x 21.
Collection of Mrs. Charles R. Henschel.

Hound and Hunter. Painted in 1891, dated 1892.
Watercolor. 13½ x 19½.
Collection of Mrs. Charles R. Henschel.

Playing Him, or The North Woods. Probably 1894.
Watercolor. 15⅛ x 21⅜.
The Currier Gallery of Art.

Camp Fire, Adirondacks. Probably 1892.
Watercolor. 15 x 21-7/16.
The Art Institute of Chicago,
Mr. and Mrs. Martin A. Ryerson Collection.

The Rapids, Hudson River, Adirondacks. 1894. Watercolor. 15⅛ x 21½. The Art Institute of Chicago, Mr. and Mrs. Martin A. Ryerson Collection.

Adirondack Guide. 1894. Watercolor. 15 x 21¼.
Museum of Fine Arts, Boston.

The Artist's Studio in an Afternoon Fog. 1894. Oil. 23⅞ x 30¼.
Memorial Art Gallery of the University of Rochester.

The Fox Hunt. 1893. Oil. 38 x 68. Pennsylvania Academy of the Fine Arts.

Below Zero. 1894. Oil. 24 x 28. Yale University Art Gallery.

A Light on the Sea. 1897. Oil. 28¼ x 48¼. The Corcoran Gallery of Art.

Cannon Rock. 1895. Oil. 39-3/16 x 39⅛. The Metropolitan Museum of Art.

OPPOSITE: *The Lookout—"All's Well".* 1896. Oil. 40 x 30¼. Museum of Fine Arts, Boston.

Watching the Breakers: A High Sea. 1896. Oil. 24⅛ x 38¼. Canajoharie Library and Art Gallery.

The Wreck. 1896. Oil. 30 x 48. Museum of Art, Carnegie Institute.

On a Lee Shore. 1900. Oil. 39 x 39. Museum of Art, Rhode Island School of Design.

Young Ducks. 1897. Watercolor. 14 x 21.
Private Collection.

Montagnais Indians. 1895. Watercolor.
13½ x 19¾. Collection of Howard N. Garfinkle.

Ouananiche Fishing. 1897.
Watercolor. 14 x 20¾.
Museum of Fine Arts, Boston.

Lake St. John, or Lake Shore. 1895.
Watercolor. 14½ x 20.
The Paine Art Center and Arboretum.

The Guide. 1895. Watercolor. 13½ x 19⅝. Collection of George D. Hart.

Rum Cay. Probably 1898 or 1899. Watercolor. 14-15/16 x 21⅜. Worcester Art Museum.

The Turtle Pound. 1898. Watercolor. 14-15/16 x 21⅜. The Brooklyn Museum.

After the Tornado. 1899. Watercolor. 14-15/16 x 21⅜. The Art Institute of Chicago, Mr. and Mrs. Martin A. Ryerson Collection.

The Coming Storm. 1901. Watercolor. 14-7/16 x 21-1/16. Collection of Mrs. Charles R. Henschel.

West India Divers. 1899.
Watercolor. 15 x 21½.
The University of Kansas Museum of Art.

Under the Coco Palm. 1898.
Watercolor. 14⅝ x 20⅞. Fogg Art Museum.

The Gulf Stream. 1899. Oil. 28⅛ x 49⅛. The Metropolitan Museum of Art.

West Point, Prout's Neck, Maine. 1900. Oil. 30¼ x 48¼. Sterling and Francine Clark Art Institute.

Searchlight, Harbor Entrance, Santiago de Cuba. 1901. Oil. 30⅝ x 50½. The Metropolitan Museum of Art.

North Road, Bermuda. 1900.
Watercolor. 13⅝ x 20⅞.
Collection of Mrs. John Wintersteen.

In the Jungle, Florida. 1904.
Watercolor. 13⅞ x 19⅝.
The Brooklyn Museum.

Diamond Shoal. 1905. Watercolor. 13½ x 21¼. IBM Corporation.

Kissing the Moon. 1904. Oil. 30 x 40. Addison Gallery of American Art.

Cape Trinity, Saguenay River. 1904. Oil. 28¾ x 48¾. Collection of Alastair Bradley Martin.

Right and Left. 1909. Oil. 28¼ x 48½. National Gallery of Art.

Driftwood. 1909. Oil. 24¼ x 28. Collection of Dr. and Mrs. S. Emlen Stokes.

List of Illustrations

Oils

An Adirondack Lake. Henry Gallery, University of Washington, Seattle, Washington. 60.

The Artist's Studio in an Afternoon Fog. Memorial Art Gallery of the University of Rochester, R. T. Miller Fund. 106.

Autumn. Collection of Mr. and Mrs. Paul Mellon. 81.

Beach Scene. Private Collection. 61.

Below Zero. Yale University Art Gallery, Bequest of George Roberts. 108.

Breezing Up, or A Fair Wind. National Gallery of Art, Gift of the W. L. and May T. Mellon Foundation. 77.

The Bridle Path, White Mountains. Sterling and Francine Clark Art Institute. 58.

The Bright Side. Private Collection, New York. 52.

Butterflies. The New Britain Museum of American Art. 82.

Cannon Rock. The Metropolitan Museum of Art, Gift of George A. Hearn, 1906. 110.

Cape Trinity, Saguenay River. Collection of Alastair Bradley Martin. 129.

The Carnival. The Metropolitan Museum of Art, Purchase, Lazarus Fund, 1922. 79.

The Country School. The St. Louis Art Museum. 57.

Croquet Scene. The Art Institute of Chicago. 55.

Watercolors

Harrowing. Collection of Mr. and Mrs. James W. Titelman. 86.

Hound and Hunter. Collection of Mrs. Charles R. Henschel. 102.

In the Jungle, Florida. The Brooklyn Museum. 126.

Lake St. John, or Lake Shore. The Paine Art Center and Arboretum, Oshkosh, Wisconsin. 116.

Leaping Trout. Museum of Fine Arts, Boston, William Wilkins Warren Fund. 98.

Looking over the Cliff. Plainfield Public Library, Plainfield, N.J. 87.

Montagnais Indians. Collection of Howard N. Garfinkle. 115.

A "Norther," Key West. Private Collection, New York. 96.

North Road, Bermuda. Collection of Mrs. John Wintersteen. 126.

Ouananiche Fishing. Museum of Fine Arts, Boston, William Wilkins Warren Fund. 116.

Playing Him, or The North Woods. The Currier Gallery of Art, Manchester, N.H. 103.

The Rapids, Hudson River, Adirondacks. The Art Institute of Chicago, Mr. and Mrs. Martin A. Ryerson Collection. 104.

Rum Cay. Worcester Art Museum. 118.

Drawings

Wood-Engravings

Etchings

Eight Bells. The Metropolitan Museum of Art, Dick
   Fund, 1941. 40.

Mending the Tears. The Metropolitan Museum of Art,
   Dick Fund, 1941. 42.

Perils of the Sea. The Metropolitan Museum of Art,
   Dick Fund, 1941. 43.

Saved. The Metropolitan Museum of Art, Dick Fund,
   1924. 44.